BRAND U

REIMAGINING WHO YOU ARE

RON NORMAN

Palmetto Publishing Group, LLC

Palmetto Publishing Group, LLC
Charleston, SC

For more information regarding special discounts for bulk purchases, please contact Palmetto Publishing Group at Info@PalmettoPublishingGroup.com.

ISBN-13: 978-1-944313-29-6
ISBN-10: 1-944313-29-X

To my amazing mom, Margaret Norman, who I love so dearly. Thank you so much for your support. Momma, we did it! I couldn't have made it to this point without your support and encouragement. Thank you for introducing me to Christ and for showing me how to be a Christian through the way you live your life.

To my dad, Ronald Norman Sr., and my brother, Micaiah Norman, thank you both for your support. You all have helped me become the man I am today. I love you!

To my grandma, Rosa Mae Norman, thank you for your unwavering love and support. You have watched me grow throughout the years and have always remained by my side. You are truly the rock of our family. I love you!

TABLE OF CONTENTS

INTRODUCTION

For we are His workmanship, created in Christ Jesus unto good works, which God hath before ordained that we should walk in them.

—Eph. 2:10 (KJV)

Let's imagine there's a CEO who oversees the production of billions of products at his company; we'll call the company Kingdom Business, Inc. At this company, the CEO single-handedly designs and creates each of those products for his own personal use. Furthermore, the CEO built Kingdom Business, Inc. in just six days. Amazing, huh?

As you may have guessed, this is no ordinary CEO—this CEO is God, and we are the billions of products He has created. We are all exceptionally made, each of us with our own special features and specifications.

Product Specifications

Our gifts and talents are what make us unique. We all look and speak differently, but what differentiates us even more are our gifts. Whatever comes naturally to you is a gift. Whether you are athletic, you can sing really well, or cook like nobody's business, you were designed to share your gifts to glorify God. Our gifts will ultimately lead us to our purpose in life. Everyone is created with a purpose. God makes no mistakes. It's our task to discover our purpose in order to fulfill it. Yes, this is easier said than done.

Have you ever prayed to God and asked Him to reveal His purpose for your life? Rather than getting the audible or visual confirmation you expected, were you met with silence, or even worse, uncertainty? If so, I can relate! What I've learned is that God will not reveal His purpose for us all at once, but He will do so over time. Our purpose is our treasure, and it would be unfortunate for us to give up before we realize our individual purpose.

Know Your Brand

Companies like Apple and Nike have formed billion-dollar corporations by staying consistent in terms of their branding. The founders of these corporations discovered a niche in the market and produced premium products to cater to those customers. These products are representative of the companies' missions to be innovative, groundbreaking, and transformative. The Nike "swoosh" and the bitten apple logo are recognizable around the world. Even if you've never tried any of the products, you've probably seen them.

We are all representatives of our manufacturer: God. He has designed and sculpted us in His image for a specific purpose. Although we are all created by God, not everyone is branded as one of His children. If you are fortunate to have been branded as a Child of God, you must realize the power you possess. In 1 Peter 2:9–10 (MSG), we are reminded of this: "[We] are the ones chosen by God, chosen for the high calling of priestly work, chosen to be a holy people, God's instruments to do His work and speak out for Him, to tell others of the night-and-day difference he made for you—from nothing to something, from rejected to accepted." You are unlike the rest of the crowd, so you must stand boldly to affirm who you are and to whom you belong.

Lifetime Warranty

God insures us with a lifetime warranty! This protection policy covers us for the rest of our lives. Jesus suffered and died at Calvary to pay the price for our sins, which can never be repaid. Like any CEO, God wants His products to perform at their greatest potential. He values us so much, and wants us to be handled with the utmost care. Although there will be people who'll try to harm us, we are all given an owner's manual that shows us how to handle any circumstances that may come our way. Our owner's manual is the Holy Bible, and the term "Bible" can be thought of as an acronym, as it contains our *Basic Instructions Before Leaving Earth.* Our journeys may be different, but the Bible is applicable to all of our lives.

Batteries Included

God not only sends us into the world with the necessary basic instructions, but He also equips us with enough battery life to sustain us during our journey. Faith is that power source. We can tap into it whenever we are feeling low, fearful, or unsure of our future. There is an abundant supernatural supply; all we need is a small amount—about the size of a mustard seed—and with this we are able to move mountains (Matt. 17:20 MSG). Faith is that driving force that moves us forward along our journey of self-discovery. This process includes:

- DISCOVERING OUR BRAND. Our brand is the promise of who we are. Knowing what we represent will have a huge impact on how we view ourselves, and how we handle situations.

- ANSWERING THE CALL. You must first posture yourself to be called. Be in constant communication with God through prayer and meditation. His still, small voice will help you understand the reason you are here.

- FULFILLING GOD'S MASTER PLAN. God intends for us to be successful. He has called us for a specific purpose, and the responsibility is on us to bring that purpose to fruition. His plans for us will supersede any dreams we could possibly dream for ourselves.

- UNDERGOING PRODUCTION. We are equipped to endure the hard times and the setbacks of life. God allows for us to be tested so we can prove our durability. When we are tested, God gives us an opportunity to grow. We can't grow unless we are challenged.

- ACTIVATING OUR FAITH. Faith in our brand is the driving force that propels us to our destiny. If we don't activate our faith, we aren't going anywhere. James 2:26 (KJV) says, "Faith without works is dead!"

- MARKETING OUR BRAND. We must proudly proclaim the brand we represent. We are not asked to be boastful, but unashamed. Let your brand shine through the way you live your life.

- BOUGHT WITH A PRICE. We are not our own. We were bought. Jesus paid by making the ultimate sacrifice when He died for us—He will supply all of our needs.

- SENT BACK TO THE MANUFACTURER. If we are ever broken, worn out, or have lost our way, God will always be there to welcome us back with open arms.

Before you begin this journey, be honest with yourself about where you are now on this path, and be clear about the type of person you would like to become. This internal dialogue will help you understand that you have a brand. Discover your brand and use it as inspiration to carry you through your path to your destiny. Your brand is greater than yourself because you're meant to make an impact in the world and be used as a conduit for Kingdom Business, Inc.

CHAPTER 1

DISCOVERING YOUR BRAND

Your very lives are a letter that anyone can read by just looking at you. Christ himself wrote it—not with ink, but with God's living Spirit; not chiseled into stone, but carved into human lives—and we publish it.

—2 Cor. 3:1–3 (MSG)

The person I wanted to become when I grew up was unlike any person I had ever met. Yes, there were people whom I looked up to and who inspired me, but they weren't doing what I wanted to do. No matter how far-fetched it seemed, I wanted to be someone who entertained and inspired millions. Growing up, make-believe was often considered to be my playtime. Either I was learning new magic tricks from the tutorial VHS cassette tape that I got in a kit, or I was hanging blankets

1

between doorways at the top of the stairs to pretend I was a performer on stage. I had many dreams that developed out of my various interests. Early on, I knew my life had a calling to do great things.

Do you remember when you were younger and your parents or guidance counselors would ask, "What do you want to be when you grow up?" Maybe you had some lofty or ambitious dreams that you knew without a shadow of a doubt would come true someday. Do you still have those dreams, or have they changed? If you're like me, your dreams have probably changed over time. It's okay; it may mean that your interests changed after you were exposed to new things. Whatever the case, I hope it isn't because you gave up. God gives us dreams to direct us to our purpose. It may be unclear now which profession(s) you will ultimately pursue, but hopefully you have an idea of where your passions lie. Every fulfilling career taps into a person's passions. Whether you want to be a teacher who enjoys shaping the minds of our future leaders, or an attorney who believes justice should be upheld—you are motivated by your passions.

There were several times in my life when I would question myself, and even God, while trying to figure out my purpose in life. Why was I created? It wasn't that I questioned my existence, but I just wanted to know what I should be doing to live out the purpose God had ordained for me. Many of us are seeking purpose and meaning in life; I'm here to encourage you to be patient. You don't have to figure it out right now. Discovering your purpose is a process that comes only from being in tune with the Father and having a relationship with Him.

So why does God withhold such vital information from us? How are we supposed to know which direction to go in if God doesn't fill us in on our assignment? Life is a journey, and during this journey, God prepares us for what he has set aside for us. Your purpose is not a secret, but your treasure. What do you enjoy? What makes you angry? These could be good indicators of what your purpose involves. How to go about finding your purpose could be right under your nose!

Know Who You Represent

To know your brand is to be aware of who you really are. I'm not talking about your title or your role—or even who you claim to be—but your true, authentic self. Who are you when you're all alone and no one else is looking? This may seem like a deep philosophical question, but it doesn't have to be. We are the souls of God. Our lives are branded by our Manufacturer. We are created to live a life that pleases Him.

Have I always been confident, strong in my faith, and sure of myself? Absolutely not! I still go through times when I question my abilities and my faith. But I'm encouraged to know that I am who I am today because God touched my heart and gave me something greater than myself to live for.

We cannot fulfill our purpose or maximize our potential until we discover who we are. If you accept Jesus Christ as your Lord and Savior, you are a Child of God. As a Child of God you're destined to do great things for His Kingdom. You have all that you need to be successful inside of you. The Bible says, ". . . greater is He that is in you, than he that is in the world" (1 John 4:4 KJV). God is inside of you, and He will be with you always. Even if the world turns its back on you, you are still better off with God on your side.

Your brand as a Child of God means that you are precious in God's eyes, and no one can dispute that fact. Your brand has power! Being a Child of God is only the basis of who you are—like your name, for instance: You are a lot more than just your name. Your brand is multifaceted, and it's developed over time.

Have you ever noticed Twitter users' bios? Usually a person will give you a brief synopsis of who they are. My bio includes that I'm a Child of God, a son, a brother, a friend, a motivator, etc. If you could use three words to describe your brand, what would they be? Consider letting these words represent your brand; then remember to honor it. Nothing should cause you to lose the integrity of your brand.

Your brand is also made up of the relationships you keep. Whether you are a friend, son, daughter, sister, brother, mother, father, husband, or wife, your brand is enhanced by the roles you play. You can't possibly believe you only live for yourself! There are people connected to you whom you represent. They look up to you. My mother would always tell me to make good choices because my brother, Micaiah, was always watching. I wanted to set a good example for him. This held me accountable for my actions. There is always someone watching, whether you notice them or not. That's why you should have respect for yourself and for those connected to you. If you don't connect with anyone in your immediate family, find someone in your church, school, or neighborhood to hold you accountable. There has to be at least one person in your life—whether it's a teacher, pastor, coach, or mentor—whom you respect and whom you want to make proud. An accountability partner isn't someone that keeps tabs on you like a parole officer, but they help you make the right choices for your life as you pursue your dreams.

I have many mentors, some I've never even met before, who motivate me. When I find someone who embodies the qualities that I would like to emulate, I ask for a meeting, I interview them or read up on their life. Reaching out to someone from a place of respect is flattering to most people. If you find someone who's in the profession you hope to enter, don't you think it would be smart to reach out, since that person has already gone through the process? Developing these relationships could help you land a job further down the road. Be open, humble, and willing to learn.

Your professional career is also part of your brand. A career's longevity often depends upon your willingness to grow, learn, and challenge yourself. In your career, you have to go after the purpose God has assigned to you—not money. It is natural for us to long for nice things and to aim for a prestigious title or more money, but in the end, what will it all mean? There is no amount of success that can replace the value of operating within your purpose and helping others.

Insecurity Robs Us of Our Identity

As you look into the mirror, you may notice several features that you wish you could change. Maybe you think your eyes are too far apart, your nose too wide, your lips too thin—or, as in my case, your forehead too big. We perceive these things as imperfections because we are brainwashed with the idea that perfection should be staring back at us. The media clouds our minds with images of who we're supposed to be and who we're not supposed to be. Young women are told that they aren't beautiful unless they look like the women on the covers of magazines. Young men aren't seen as "real" men if they look too scrawny. How you see yourself may seem minor compared to the other issues you're dealing with. I'm not saying this to make you feel poorly about yourself; I say this to illustrate that we are all imperfect by our own standards. In Christ Jesus, we are beautifully and wonderfully made (Ps. 139:14 KJV). To know that we are made in the CEO's image, and that we are beautiful reflections of His love, should make us reconsider degrading ourselves. God makes no mistakes.

You *are* good enough! The constant yearning to be liked, understood, or reassured of your worth can be suffocating; it's like you can't breathe without this validation. How can you envision a future for yourself by seeking others' approval? We give people too much power over us. People have a way of building us up and tearing us down. The same people we call friends or loved ones are sometimes the people who hurt us the most. If this happens to you, forgive them, because they don't understand the calling God has chosen for you. Anyone who criticizes you for who you are does not understand.

The reason you stand out is because you're not like everyone else. You weren't created to fit in with the crowd; you are unique. To know that you were methodically created for this particular time and place should assure you that every test was meant to happen. God is preparing you for greater! Just like a painter's revered work of art, not everyone will understand the intentions behind the masterpiece. Consider the *Mona Lisa*, one of the greatest masterpieces of all time. Not everyone likes the painting or understands why it's famous. "What is Mona Lisa thinking?" and "Why is she smirking?" are questions that can only be answered by the artist. Similarly, there are people who will misinterpret the purpose behind the masterpieces of our lives. We are challenged on the very premise of that which makes us who we are. No, our lives aren't perfect, but if our lives are created, guided, and shaped by the hands of God, our lives will end well.

The critics are loud. When God says that you're beautiful, they'll yell, "I've seen better." Rather than listening to the voice of God, we begin to internalize the outside criticism. When people call you hurtful names, remind yourself that you are a Child of God. As a Child of God, you have the power to be more than a conqueror in Jesus Christ. When you're self-aware, small things like name-calling don't affect you as much. Yet no matter how secure you are in yourself and your faith, words can still hurt. The Bible teaches us that there is power in the tongue and that we should choose our words wisely. Although you can't control what others say or do, you can control how you treat them in return.

Growing up, I tried to ignore the hurtful names that people called me, but it still affected me. In church, my pastor would tell me that I was special and that God had called me to do great things for His Kingdom. At the time, I didn't want to stand out. I just wanted to be cool. But despite my efforts, I was still teased for being different.

I can remember a time when my cousins and I walked to our grandma's house after school with a group of girls who lived in her neighborhood. I usually didn't think about being the only guy in the group, but that particular day—I was probably eleven years old—while we were walking home, things were different.

"Why do you walk home with us? Do you not have any dude friends?" one girl asked. I had guy friends, but I didn't understand why it mattered. We were just walking home from school. It wasn't until another girl asked, "Are you a faggot?" that things changed. I was hurt. Although I didn't fully understand the meaning of the word, I knew it was an offensive term that questioned my masculinity. My cousins didn't say anything or stand up for me.

After that day, I refused to walk home with them. I would walk several yards behind them, and I thought doing so would bring me peace. But those girls would still yell and call me that same hurtful word, along with other things, and my cousins started chiming in with laughter, encouraging them to continue. Although I felt alone, I now know that I was not alone. God was with me every step of the way. He even granted me enough resolve to make it to my grandmother's house, and the wherewithal to act as if nothing had happened.

Those days had a lasting impression on me. Either I was the only guy among my cousins or the only black kid in my classes, so I never felt fully included. During this time, I allowed insecurity to cloud my judgment, and it blocked me from seeing who God called me to be. I wasn't what those kids called me, but instead of reassuring myself of that, I tried to please people. I just wanted everyone to like me. There is no peace in trying to always be a people pleaser, because you're basically becoming what everyone else wants you to be. You would have to be schizophrenic to please everybody.

Don't Allow Others to Define You

When I was younger, I was full of life and adventure. My imagination would often run rampant as I pretended to be my favorite superheroes, fighting off villains.

I was born to two loving parents who shielded me from the ills of the world. I was sheltered. I didn't understand why I couldn't stay the night over at my friends' houses. What was the big deal? My parents, both firm and caring, understood. They demonstrated the ideals of hard work, faith, and determination, and they knew to protect me when I didn't understand how to protect myself.

My dad expected the best from me. A retired command sergeant major in the US Army, he demanded that I make good grades, have perfect attendance in school, and often live out his dreams. He had been a star athlete during his high school years, and he expected me to excel in sports like he had. I enjoyed playing sports with my friends, but I lacked the athletic gene. I longed to please my dad, because despite my lack of innate athletic ability, he loved me and wanted me to excel.

When I reached a certain age, I realized I wasn't passionate about the same things he was passionate about, and I had to figure out what made me happy.

"I don't know why you want to quit basketball. You could be good if you actually practiced," my dad said.

"I really don't want to play basketball anymore. I've played for the past eight years now, and I'm tired of it," I responded.

"What about all the money I've spent on you? Bought you shoes and paid for lessons—"

"I just don't want to play anymore, all right?!" I said, interrupting him.

This was a common exchange. If it wasn't about sports, there always seemed to be something, and I felt like he often tried to use money to control me.

My mom is hardworking, selfless, and humble. A retired first-class sergeant in the US Army and a Liberty Mutual customer service representative, she set an incredible example for me. Even now, I can talk to her and confide in her when I feel at my lowest. I would talk to her about my dreams and my ideas for future professions. As I mentioned, my imagination often ran wild, so I considered an array of professions throughout the years. I imagined becoming a magician at one point, a painter at another, then a businessman, and also a gospel singer. Although my interests have changed over time, two of them have remained the same: encouraging and inspiring people.

My mom was the one who introduced me to gospel music. I would often hear it played throughout the house when she created new dances for our church dance team. I fell in love with gospel music because it uplifted me and gave me hope that everything would be fine.

At a young age, while battling self-esteem issues, I began to write songs. It was cathartic for me because I inspired myself through my lyrics. One of my first songs was called "Joyful Noise." The hook went like this:

Make a joyful noise unto the Lord!
Make a joyful noise and join the accord!
No matter how you look,
One blessing is all it took
For me to understand: He's worth the praise!

This is a simple song that inspires me still. Every day,

we should make a joyful noise unto the Lord with thanksgiving in our hearts, for He is good and worthy of being praised. Despite how we may look or feel—broken, abused, unloved, or insecure—it is the blessing of life that lets us know that He is worthy of our praise.

This song also speaks to me in another way. There is a joke in the church that goes: "It's okay if you can't sing. God just asked for us to make a joyful noise." That's true for me, because singing has never been my strong suit. Nonetheless, there was nothing I wanted more than to be a gospel singer. I would beg my mom to allow me to perform in talent shows because I knew God would open up doors of opportunity for me to advance my singing career.

One year, I asked her if I could participate in a talent showcase that she'd organized to celebrate her dance team's anniversary.

"There may not be enough time for you to perform," my mom said, subtly trying to dissuade me. She was all for my dreams, but she didn't want me to be hurt either.

"Mom, please! I've been practicing, and I'm really ready for it," I begged, and she finally relented.

The day of the showcase, I was so excited because I was about to do what I really enjoyed doing, which was ministering through song. I got up on stage to perform Yolanda Adams's "Save the World." Keep in mind that this song was performed flawlessly by one of the greatest voices of all time, and it was sung in a key beyond my range—but that didn't stop me! While performing the song, I became intimidated whenever I had to make the higher notes, so I relied on my falsetto. I *felt* that thing! I sang to the best of my ability, and after I finished the song and opened my eyes, I saw stoic looks on everyone's faces. Everyone looked like they were thinking, "What just happened?" It was at that point I realized singing may not be for me.

We are all given our own respective gifts. You are called to a specific purpose. Your purpose can't be achieved by someone else because what God has for you is for you alone. It is tailor-made to fit your unique personality traits and your custom capabilities. Be real with yourself to discover what God has in store for you. The reason you are still alive today is God's grace and mercy. His plan for your life is to bless you in ways that reflect His glory.

You can figure out your purpose by doing what comes naturally to you. Be motivated by your passions and not your wishes. What is meant for Yolanda Adams is not meant for me.

Discover Your Own Brand

You are an asset to the Kingdom of God. God has equipped you with gifts and talents to share with others.

Not everyone will understand your purpose, but don't allow others to discourage you from who God has called you to be. As a Child of God, you are purposefully made, so have faith and know that you are a limited-edition product created by God. Walking into your destiny is as simple as taking care of your "S.E.L.F.":

SURRENDER TO THE PROCESS. The journey to fulfill your destiny will not be an easy road, but there is comfort in knowing that God will direct your path and will never leave you nor forsake you. You must first surrender to His will and let God be God; give Him the wheel and let Him drive.

EVALUATE YOURSELF. Allow yourself to be subjected to your own personal evaluations. In order to grow spiritually, personally, or professionally, you must nurture the good aspects of your life and prune what's hindering you. This comes from being real with yourself and being open to constructive criticism from others. Value the opinions of your parents, close friends, or mentors if you want the best advice—not everyone wants to bring you down.

LEARN FROM YOUR MISTAKES. Mistakes remind us of our finite power. If we live long enough, we will all encounter mistakes at some point or another, and it's by

God's grace that we are able to learn from our mistakes and move forward.

FULFILL YOUR DESTINY. Every day you are a step closer to fulfilling your destiny. You must stay hungry. Go after the dreams that God has placed inside of you. You are closer to your dreams than you know.

No one knows you the way you and God know you! Do not compromise who you are because of what others may think about you. When you take care of "S.E.L.F" first, you are more focused to accomplish your mission. Don't allow temporary situations hinder you from who God has called you to be.

CHAPTER 2

ANSWER THE CALL

For I know the plans I have for you declares the Lord; plans to prosper you and not to harm you, plans to give you hope and a future.

—Jer. 29:11 (NIV)

Your calling is a divine assignment placed on your life. This is God's way of directing you to your purpose. Everyone and everything God creates has a purpose in life, but not everyone receives the call the same way. Some people may feel they heard God speak, while others may feel their calling was instinctual. Whatever the case may be, your calling is between you and God.

Pay attention to the desires, dreams, and passions that dwell inside of you. These are often good indicators of who you are called to be. Pray and ask God for His guidance, and go after your dreams. You can't accomplish anything if you aren't willing to try. If the dream doesn't pan out the way you thought it should, it's possible that God is steering you in a different direction. It isn't that you're not worthy of your dreams; it just may not be the destiny God has in mind for your life.

When I think of being called, I am reminded of the story of Moses in the Bible. Moses was minding his own business one day when God appeared to him in the form of a burning bush. To Moses's amazement, the fire did not consume the bush. God spoke to Moses, saying that He heard the cries of His people, and He wanted Moses to go and tell Pharaoh to let His people go. Moses was obviously skeptical of the whole thing. After all, what person would believe that God had spoken to them? And why would that person think God had chosen them specifically? Moses had a speech impediment, so it was tough for him to imagine delivering such a powerful statement. Moses suggested his brother, Aaron, instead, but God asked them to team up.

Moses was afraid of what people might think of him before he even got started. God said for Moses to tell the people that "I Am" had sent him, and if they still didn't believe, God told Moses to throw his rod to the ground. Moses tried it out, and his rod instantly became a serpent. Moses, frightened by this miracle, was then told to grab the serpent by its tail to get his rod back. The story goes on to say that Moses used his rod to part the Red Sea, and the children of Israel escaped Pharaoh's army safely (Exod. 14: 21–31 NIV).

The story of Moses illustrates that your purpose may be so incomprehensible that God knows you will not believe it if you hear it all at once. You might even forfeit before you begin because you feel inadequate. God assured Moses that He knew about his speech impediment. He created him. He wanted Moses to know that he would be there with him every step of the way, just as God will be for you. If God leads you to it, He will see you through it!

God has given you tools that will get you to the next level. Take a look at the resources you already have: talents, connections, finances, or education. Don't take any of these for granted because your destiny depends on them!

Never Underestimate Your Calling or the Power of God

In this day and age, it seems everyone wants to be a celebrity. Being called can be confused with thinking that status, wealth, and influence are significant. I want you to know that you are just as important as President Barack Obama, who sits behind the desk in the Oval Office; Beyoncé, who entertains thousands of people onstage; or Bishop T. D. Jakes, who ministers across the globe. Not everyone is called to become entertainers or dignitaries, but we're all called to be representatives for Christ and to love others as we would ourselves. When you underestimate your role in life, you prevent yourself from having a meaningful impact on others. This life is not about how much money you can accumulate, but how well you managed your time here on earth by utilizing the talents you have been given.

There are people whose lives are better because you are a part of them. You have to realize the value of your call. We are often so drawn to power and influence that we can't fully recognize our contributions without comparing them to others'. True success is achieved when you honor God, have compassion for others, and live out your purpose. You can't achieve success by simply mimicking what you think success looks like. Success is not the same for everyone. You can spend your life "playing" successful and miss out on your true success. Find the gifts God has placed inside of you. You are no different from other people living out their dreams. Tap into your passions, and live out your purpose. I don't believe our purpose is centered around one event or career that we're supposed to have on earth; instead, it's the totality of our life. Every moment of our life conspires to make up our purpose.

For some, it may seem they're wandering around aimlessly, trying to figure out why they were created, scouring the earth for answers. Fortunately for you, the path to your destiny is ordered by God (Ps. 37:23 KJV). It's important to remember to connect with the Father and look within to figure out your place in the world. Your brand is a guarantee that you are valuable and capable of doing great things. Don't be distracted by your current situation or people who have stood in your way. It's easy to blame others for their shortcomings' effect on your life; for example, thinking you would be better off if you had a present father or caring mother or if your biological parents hadn't placed you up for adoption. Where you are today is not by accident. God sees and knows all, and he'll be there to guide you.

The following principles describe how we can live out our best lives.

- TAP INTO YOUR CALLING. Your brand indicates that you will be called to fulfill your destiny. You have to be available to hear the call. How can you expect to receive an important call if your line is always busy? It is imperative that you are in constant communication with God. Some people say they have witnessed the voice of God directing them toward the path they were created to travel, but for me, I would pray to God for an answer, and He would always send people to confirm what I was praying about. You have to be receptive to the call.

- EXCAVATE THE GIFTS THAT ARE PLACED INSIDE OF YOU. God has placed treasures inside of you, and it's up to you to discover them. Don't be afraid to ask those close to you what your gifts are, because they may notice talents you don't see. It should be your mission in life to develop those gifts God has placed inside of you. Your gifts are specific to you, and no one can use them on your behalf. Your success comes from tapping into what comes naturally to you.

- ENHANCE YOUR BRAND. God created you as a multifaceted, complex being. You are a Child of God, and you have a calling. It's up to you to maximize what that means to you. No longer should you allow others to place limitations on who you can be—through Christ, you can do anything.

You have an opportunity now to define what God has called you to do. His plans for your life are to be used for the betterment of His Kingdom. You are an asset to Christ, and it's up to you to respond to the call. Your response can be as simple as telling God yes. You're saying yes to allowing God to come into your life and yes to being used by Him.

CHAPTER 3

FULFILLING GOD'S MASTER PLAN

Only God . . . makes things grow. The one who plants and the one who waters have one purpose . . . for we are coworkers in God's service.

—1 Cor. 3:7–9 (NIV)

Most business plans begin as a design or an idea in an innovator's mind. The inventor recognizes a need and develops a product or service for monetary gain and/or for the greater good. God sees needs in the world, and He creates people like you and me to carry out His business plan for the good of His people.

God has called you, Child of God, to go witness to others so the gospel of Jesus Christ is spread throughout the world. You may not have a global ministry, but you can be a witness through the way you live your life. Great or small, you have a purpose. God uses your purpose to show His divinity here on earth. Martin Luther King, Jr. said, "If a man is called to be a street sweeper, he should sweep streets even as a Michelangelo painted, or Beethoven composed music or Shakespeare wrote poetry. He should sweep streets so well that all the hosts of heaven and earth will pause to say, 'Here lived a great street sweeper who did his job well.'" Your current profession may not be your calling, but while you have this position, you should do your best and give God praise for the opportunity. It's only a matter of time before you discover your purpose and ultimately live out your destiny.

Before you were born, God knew your purpose. He gave you all of the necessary tools to be successful. Your personality, talent, and creativity are examples of these tools. Your tools are developed through your life experiences, such as disappointments or achievements. You can use these experiences when sharing your testimony to inspire others. Your testimony and your purpose go hand in hand. Your purpose is what you are ultimately striving to discover, and your testimony is a record of what you had to go through to get there.

How You Live Today Will Shape
Your Tomorrow

Operating within your purpose requires discipline, making good decisions, and sacrifice. The saying "Anything in life that is worth having is worth fighting for" is more than just a saying—it's a way of life. If you are a Child of God, you have to live for Him and follow the example Jesus has set for us. Is this challenging? Of course! But it's our duty to stand boldly and show the world who we represent. It's easy to accept God's blessings, but to acknowledge your relationship with Him is a different story. Christianity has become a taboo topic because society suggests it's best to keep your faith to yourself to avoid offending someone.

When I was in school, I straddled the fence of faith and "worldly" living. I knew if I opened up about my faith, I would be perceived as a goody two-shoes who would never step foot into a party. If I came across as worldly, then I would compromise the values in the core of my being. I found it easier to just keep my faith to myself. Now I know God is not some statue we can pull out of the closet and worship when it's convenient. We serve a living God who wants a real relationship with us.

Being who you truly are can be tough. You are expected to have everything figured out at an early age: whom you should be friends with, the types of clothes you should wear, and whom you should love. During your teenage years, you may think you know everything, but it's important to realize there's still a lot to learn. Yes, you are no longer a baby under your parent's constant supervision, but you aren't quite an adult yet either. It's interesting how as teenagers we can know so much, but struggle with our self-identity at the same time. You may be convinced that the path to manhood or womanhood is to fall into stereotypical teen behaviors or thoughts. These are all ploys to rob you of who you are destined to become. Don't allow someone to define you. Those same people who have an opinion about you probably don't have a clue about who they are.

My insecurities as a child fueled my desire to fit in as a teenager. It took me a while to finally figure out how to be me. I often felt lonely. I didn't love myself enough to find peace in my alone time. I often had shallow friendships because I expected my friends to give me something: validation, confidence, acceptance, etc. Often my "best friends" were people I had little to nothing in common with, but we were friends because they were willing to hang out. They made me feel accepted. I wanted to know that I was good enough, but to do that, I placed a huge burden on others, and that was unfair. People can't define you or give you inner peace. You need something more substantial. Look no further than Jesus Christ. Even in romantic relationships, we cannot expect our significant other to complete us. Life is all about growth, and we can often learn from the people we date, but we shouldn't compromise our self-worth or morals to be with someone.

While in college, I dated several women just to have someone. One woman in particular, named Savannah, was beautiful, intelligent, and funny; we met through a mutual friend. Savannah and I started as friends, but she wanted to take our relationship to the next level. She went to another school, so making time for her became a challenge. Late one night, she called me and asked, "So what are we doing?" Sarcastically, I responded, "We're talking." She replied, "No, I mean, this has gone on long enough, and you're either going to date me or you're not."

I did have feelings for her, but I wasn't mature enough to say that. I just wanted her to fill a void in my life. I enjoyed talking to her, but I knew this couldn't go on the way it had been. Before I could respond to her question, most likely with an excuse, she said, "You make time for what you want to make time for." She was right. There was no reason for me to continue stringing her along if I wasn't planning on taking our relationship seriously.

I learned a valuable lesson from that conversation. I shouldn't allow my insecurity to be the reason I hold on to someone. She deserved so much more than that. I needed to allow myself time to mature before I sought a relationship with someone else.

Experience Is the Best Teacher

We can often find ourselves doing things we know we don't have any business doing. Our parents can show us the way, but we have to learn things on our own. Despite our poor choices, God is with us the entire time. He looks beyond our faults and directs us down the right path.

If you are a diligent follower of Jesus Christ, he will reward your faithfulness. When you are deliberate about your relationship with Christ, he will be a great counselor, guide, and friend. God wants to meet you in the proverbial "boardroom" to discuss your life. You don't need a physical boardroom; all you need to do is get down on your knees and pray—God is always listening. In the boardroom, you and God can discuss the next steps in fulfilling your destiny. God is personally invested in you, and He wants the product of your life to be significant. You are not created just to survive, but to live a noteworthy life. As a product of God, you are more than just a novelty He has created. He has appointed you as the manager of your life. Why wouldn't you consult with the CEO who created you?

I know how easy it is to get out of sync with the Father. Our daily lives can distract us from finding time to pray or meditate. When you seek God on a daily basis, "the peace of God that passes all understanding will guard your heart and your mind" (Phil. 4:7 NIV).

As the manager of your life, you are given free rein to make your own decisions. God has placed dreams inside of you, and it's up to you to fulfill them. God is not some genie who will make your visions become reality. He expects a conscientious effort on your part, which should include making the right decisions. Are you confident that amidst temptation you will always make the right decisions? If you answered yes, then this book is not for you. I, along with so many others, wrestle with cravings, compulsions, or selfish desires on a daily basis. Rather than being led by the spirit, we may give in to those urges. We are human, and we are prone to making mistakes. Mistakes are wake-up calls to get you back on track. We can choose to allow a mistake to deter us from our journey, or we can learn from the error and keep moving.

As you wear your brand—Child of God—God is marketing you as more than a conquerer, the head and not the tail, the first and not the last, a lender and not a borrower (Deut. 28:13 KJV). But do you follow your calling? God has called you to live your best life, which begins with the renewal of your mind. God has already told us who we are, but the devil tries to challenge that. The devil reminds us of our past mistakes and attempts to showcase our inabilities to manipulate us. It's his job to seek "whom he may devour," so don't give in (1 Pet. 5:8 KJV). The devil is a liar.

I know your struggle may seem difficult, but you are not in this fight alone. It is your task to seek God daily in prayer and feed your spirit with His word for protection. Also, be courageous enough to talk with a parent, mentor, or someone you trust and respect. True healing comes from expressing how you feel and being transparent about your problems. You're not the first person to think these thoughts.

Despite your current situation in life, don't give up on God, because He will not give up on you. You may be struggling with accepting who you are. During your whole life, people may have neglected you, called you out by name, or reaffirmed those inner thoughts that have you bound. Do you put your trust in people, or do you put your trust in God? God is there with you every step of the way. He will never leave you or forsake you (Deut. 31:6 KJV). He cares so deeply for you and only wants to see you fulfill your destiny.

Surrendering to the Process

God requires that you surrender your life to Him. Your life is not your own; it belongs to the Lord. Before we even begin perfecting our products, we must surrender to God's plan for our lives and trust the process. How much we're willing to trust Him will determine how far we'll go.

In the sixth grade, my teacher, Mrs. Lassiter, pulled me aside while my classmates and I made our way back inside after recess. Nervously, I got out of line to see what I had done.

"Ronald, have you heard about the student council elections?" she asked.

"I heard the announcement, but I'm not interested," I responded.

"Well, give it some thought. You would be really great at it," she said.

I appreciated her encouragement, but who was I kidding? I was terrified of speaking in public. I didn't want to give the other students something to ridicule me about. It was easier for me to play it cool and fly under the radar. In order to campaign for student council, I knew I would have to write and recite a speech in front of my entire grade. My gift is that I am very personable and I can relate to different people, but speaking in front of a crowd was too intimidating.

After giving it some thought, I decided to run for sixth-grade vice president. My mom was my biggest supporter. She helped me design posters and ribbons for my campaign. She and I even created a felt banner that hung down vertically from a wooden rod. It was totally different from everyone else's posters, which helped me stand out. Campaigning and creating posters was the easy part. What I dreaded most was having to make a speech in front of my peers.

The day finally came for me to make my speech, and I was terrified. After two of my opponents recited their speeches, it was my turn. I stood there, looked out over the audience, and then looked down at my paper. "Here goes nothing," I thought. As I stood there at the podium, I hoped my voice wasn't trembling as much as my hand was. Once I finished reciting my speech, my classmates cheered so loudly for me. This was new for me—it was a rush that I fell in love with. It not only solidified for me that I was good at something, but it also assured me that I could do anything I set my mind to. I just had to put in hard work and surrender to the process. After the election, I was pronounced the winner. The position didn't award me any special privileges, but I gained confidence and I finally found something I was passionate about. If I had allowed my fear to prevent me from trying something different, I would have missed out on something that I enjoyed.

Surrendering is a part of the process. In order to accomplish any goal in life, there's a part of you that has to step aside and let God do His part. I am someone who likes to be in control, but what I have grown to realize is that God's plan is never anything I can figure out.

His plans for us were organized before we were even born. God knew who you would become. No matter the obstacles you face, know that you have been PLANned (Purposefully Led Against Negativity). You have to look beyond your shortcomings, and where you think you should be, to find the good in your journey.

CHAPTER 4

UNDERGOING PRODUCTION

And we knew that in all things God works for the good of those who love Him, who have been called according to His purpose.

—Rom. 8:28 (KJV)

Everything must go through a maturation process. Whether you consider the saplings that eventually become strong trees, or the trajectory of your life, everything undergoes development. God created the heavens and the earth during a six-day process. God is all-powerful, and He could have created the world in a day, but instead He demonstrated how things are built in stages.

Products begin as a design. Before a product is distributed for sale, it undergoes tests that are meant to access the product's performance under pressure. If the product breaks down, the inventor will make the necessary adjustments to improve the product. You are tested on a regular basis to bring out the best in you. Tests aren't meant to harm you, but to demonstrate your durability—to give you the opportunity to access what you've learned and see your faith in action.

As long as you live, you will undergo production. It's a gradual process that prepares us for the various stages of life. Production can be the most frustrating and uncertain time in our lives. God, unfortunately, doesn't give us an itinerary to show us how long we'll have to experience a particular period of production before we can move on to the next one. Each stage is not allotted the same period of time. One level of production may last only a week, and another may take years. Production requires patience and trust.

Production is a process that keeps us growing and maturing in order to be more like Christ. God is well aware of our capabilities and will promote us when it's our time. The Bible says, "They that wait on the Lord shall renew their strength" (Isa. 40:31 KJV). Take a little time to appreciate the progress you've made so far. You are not where you started! While you're celebrating, don't become complacent, but keep striving. The vision that God has given you will come to pass. It is up to you to undergo production, not necessarily understanding the vision. God wants to use your story for His glory to show others that all things are possible through Him.

What Binds You Will Release You

A test has an expiration date; it is not meant to last always. God is simply developing you to withstand greater challenges. I don't mean to diminish your struggles, but our tests are all relative. They're never as great as they seem. Not every struggle is a fight. The opposing forces will try to deter you from your mission, but you have an unfair advantage over any struggle. God has granted you favor over your life, and if you turn your battles over to Him, He will fight them for you. God is undefeated and will never lose a fight. If you allow Him, He will step into your situation, and you will win. Favor ain't fair! You will receive your breakthrough from whatever binds you!

To put it simply: giving in to self-doubt and insecurity is what binds you, but overcoming them is how you get your release. You cannot receive release from holding on to past events and past hurts. Things that were said to me at twelve years old still affect me today, but I will not let those words hinder me. It took me a long time to understand that self-esteem is not based on the opinions others hold of me. Self-esteem is how I view myself.

When you have access to the Father, you have access to His favor. No man or woman declaring God as the Lord of Lords and King of Kings is void of favor. Favor is a divine gift that cannot be repaid. As you look back over your life, you will notice some "favor moments." No matter how bleak your situation, think back to a time when God sent someone to your rescue at your darkest hour. Whether it was a monetary gift, or food, or just words of encouragement, God was there for you. You are highly favored, and it is by God's grace and mercy that you are here today.

Have you ever been under-qualified for a position, but you got the job anyway? That's favor. Have you ever avoided what could have been a dangerous accident? That's favor. God will bypass your mess and will bless you anyway. There's nothing we can do to earn God's favor because we don't deserve it. We are all favored at different levels, but God is just, and He does not want any of us to go lacking. It doesn't mean one person is loved more by God than another. It simply means that your favor matches your calling. You may look at some- one else's blessing and wonder why God didn't bless you similarly. Your neighbor's blessing wasn't meant for you. When God blesses you, that blessing is prepackaged with your name on it. Be mindful of becoming envi- ous of someone else's blessing. You never know what that person had to sacrifice or had to go through to get to the point they're at. If God is blessing your neighbor, then He's in the neighborhood. Be grateful for what you have and where you are.

As mentioned earlier, when I was younger, the adults at my church would often tell me, "The favor of God is all over your life, young man." At the time, I didn't think I was special or any different from anyone else. This prophecy became a little more obvious when I found myself in situations that could have consumed me, but God brought me out every time. Although we know that God will bring us out of certain situations, it shouldn't be the reason we put ourselves in predicaments that could end badly. I have made many dumb mistakes in my life. For instance, one night I was hanging out on my college campus with nothing to do. I reached out to some of my friends who went to a nearby college to see what they were doing. It was already late, so I knew if I sat around a little longer, I'd fall asleep. My friends replied to my text, saying they were going out to a club and were pre-gaming at one of their apartments. I drove over, and immediately I was given drinks. We were drinking and having a good time. It was already almost one in the morning. Not only was I tipsy, but I was also feeling sleepy again.

One of the guys who wasn't drinking offered to be our designated driver to the club. Around 4:00 a.m., we got back in the guy's car and rode back to my friend's apartment. Once we made it back, everyone walked to their respective apartments. I was offered the couch at my friend's place, but I wanted to get back to my own bed. I thought I would be fine since my college was only ten minutes away. I got in my car and headed back to school. Drunk and drowsy, I couldn't wait to get back to my room. At one point, I was on the highway and I felt myself dozing off. I rolled down the windows and blasted the music, but even that didn't work. I fell asleep behind the wheel and was awakened by an abrupt BOOM! As you would imagine, I was panicking. I had hit the curb, and I was two feet away from hitting a lamppost. I was terrified because I had damaged my car. What would my parents think? I made the decision to drive the car back to campus, broken axle and busted tire in tow.

I couldn't believe the danger I had put myself in, and I couldn't thank anyone but God for bringing me out of that situation without so much as a scratch. Even when I was in the wrong, God still kept me safe. Things could have turned out a whole lot worse. I am so thankful for the favor God has placed over my life. I'm not trying to glamorize drunk driving or convince you that God will prevent you from ever getting hurt. I'm simply saying this: don't allow yourself to get out of sync with God. God may take something from you or place you in certain situations to grab your attention. God wants a relationship with you. There should never be a barrier between you and God. No matter what situations we find ourselves in, or how far away we drift from God, He will be right there with us every step of the way.

Let It Go

During production, you may have to downsize. When you surrender your life to Christ, you will have to make some tough decisions and give up some things. You can be bogged down with friends who don't have your best interests at heart, or involved in "recreational activities" that could harm you. God wants to elevate you, but if you're carrying too much weight, how can He? Let go of anything that doesn't bring you closer to God, and get out of your own way. Yes, your growth can be stifled by your own actions.

Before I got my college acceptance letter, I was a little uneasy because some of my friends had already received their letters. I knew I didn't have anything to worry about, but it was the uncertainty of not knowing.

The night I finally got my letter, my family and I were relaxing in the living room watching TV. My dad was lying on the couch, slowly dozing off, and I was sitting in the recliner.

"Hey Dad, have you checked the mailbox yet?" I asked.

"Nope, I sure didn't," he said nonchalantly.

I didn't bother to ask my mom because she rarely checked the mail. I got up and walked down the driveway to grab the mail. Among all of the bills and advertisements, I saw the letter from Wofford. It was a thick packet, so I assumed it was an acceptance letter. I got back inside, sat down at the kitchen bar, and opened the letter. It said: "We are pleased to congratulate you and welcome you into the class of 2013." I shouted to my parents, who were in the next room. My dad got up from the couch and began to read it for himself. He then lifted me up and chanted, "Sherman, Sherman, Sherman" (a reference to *The Nutty Professor*), embarrassing me. My brother, Micaiah, ran downstairs to see what all the commotion was about, and he pretended not to care. I gave my mom a hug. My parents were overjoyed!

This event meant a great deal because I would be the first in my family to attend college. Beyond this, I was so excited to finally go to college. I had a terrible case of growing pains, and I was so ready to get out of the house. I had been saving for college since I was fifteen years old, working at my first job as a fry cook at a restaurant in my hometown. I didn't enjoy working there, but I enjoyed making money. After a year at the restaurant, I took a different job at a grocery store and worked there throughout high school. I managed to save over $8,000, which I planned to put toward my college tuition.

When I received my first tuition bill, it included all the scholarships I'd received, including the Bonner Scholarship, a community-service-based scholarship that had required 280 hours of community service each year and 280 hours over two summers. I enjoyed doing community service, so I had accepted the challenge. My tuition bill left a remaining balance of about $8,000 I would still have to pay, so it would wipe out my savings. I didn't mind paying my tuition for the first semester, but what about the other seven? I asked my dad if he could help, and things changed. He was no longer chanting "Sherman, Sherman, Sherman." I asked him several times before I realized I would have to continue working part-time at the grocery store to save for the next semester. My mom helped pay for my books.

My first semester of college was exciting and stressful at the same time. I was excited to finally be away from home (although I was only twenty minutes away) and excited to meet new friends. That same excitement was paired with the stress of not knowing how I would pay for the next semester's tuition. Saving money for tuition became my primary focus. Making friends and schoolwork came next. My priorities were in that order, which was a poor decision on my part. I continued to work because I didn't want to depend on my parents for money. I worked fifteen hours a week, joined several clubs and organizations, and then I took eighteen credit hours. I had a full plate. That semester, I did poorly and came out with a whopping 1.56 GPA, and I was placed on academic probation. I had never made grades like that before.

Also, during that semester, a few people I called "friends" constantly let me down. I ended up distancing myself from them, and I started doing my own thing. This period was a dark time for me, because I didn't know where I could turn. I watched all my plans dissolve, but God had everything under control. Our lives are divinely orchestrated, and there is nothing that surprises God. In my naïveté, I thought I could plan my college experience. There is a joke that says, "If you want to make God laugh, just tell Him your plans."

Despite all of the worrying, God made a way for me. The next semester and the semesters following, my mom gave me a gift of $2,000 to go toward my tuition. Not only that, my college worked with me to recalculate my financial aid. There was an error with my "family contribution estimate" that cost me $8,000, and I was able to get it all back. I was even able to work only a day each week at my job—I am still surprised they let me do that. My dad eventually came around and started to give me $100 every now and again to be used as some extra spending money.

God took me through that test to show me that I can trust Him. There is nothing too hard for my God. My stress only made things worse. Instead of trying to figure it out, I should have surrendered to God's will. My mom even tried to assure me that everything would work out. She joked that she would sell the house to pay for my college education if she had to. Rather than allowing people to help, I was trying to be my own man. I learned from this experience that it's okay to ask for help when you need it. You can never be so strong or independent that you can't use someone's help.

God has possibly had to bring you out of a similar situation. It's not that He is a cruel God, but He knew you could handle it. Whatever it is, God brought you through it, and you are a survivor. The reason you are here today is because God kept you and knew you still have work left to do.

As crazy as this may sound, your life is not about you. You can be as successful in your career and as wealthy as you want to be, but that is not the definition of "the good life." The good life is living your life for Christ and using your testimony to inspire others. People need to know that no matter how bleak their situations seem, there is a God that is capable of bringing them out. You are needed now more than ever! God has entrusted you with your purpose, and He is pruning you to operate at your greatest potential. God provides you with trials to develop those gifts that were placed inside of you.

Everything Works Together for Your Good

Everything that God has promised you is yours. You will not receive what God has for you by sitting on the couch and allowing life to pass you by. You have to work toward your destiny. No, you may not know the destination, but God has given you glimpses of your future. Your dreams are those glimpses that'll assure you that you won't always be in this same predicament. You have to do the work and train to get where you want to be. Once God sees that you are committed and faithful, He will elevate you. The Bible says, "Faith without works is dead" (James 2:20 KJV).

After my terrible first semester of college, I knew I could do better, and I wanted to be better. I worked hard to get my priorities in check and began exploring ideas I had for my future. I was still unsure of what I wanted to major in or do after college, but I didn't want to sit back and wait for an epiphany. I got out there and tried new things. At one point, I thought I would become an attorney, so I planned to double major in government and business economics. I was fortunate to land an internship at a law firm in town, and the people there were awesome, but I quickly realized that a career in law wasn't what I wanted to do. I blame Hollywood for glamorizing the law profession. I also focused and increased my GPA to a 3.31 the second semester. I was finally getting myself together, but I still felt alone. I had friends, and we would hang out on occasion, but they had joined fraternities or had other friend groups; so I tried to find other things to occupy my time.

Wofford College had a strong Greek presence. I knew I wanted to join a fraternity, but I didn't feel that the fraternities on campus suited my interests. There were only Interfraternity Council fraternities and two National Pan-Hellenic Council fraternities. After doing some research, I found out Phi Beta Sigma was offered at a neighboring college and allowed Wofford students to join. There had never been a Sigma man on Wofford's campus before I came around. I went through the process and met three great guys who became my fraternity brothers: Oscar Dobson, Aaron Pellot, and Fredrick Harrison. Although these guys went to a neighboring school, we became close friends. We supported each other, and of course we attended each other's school parties.

Now a Bonner Scholar, Phi Beta Sigma fraternity member—also a member of a host of other organizations—and most importantly, a student, I had a lot on my plate once again. I still had the desire to do more. I had a dream of becoming the student-body president.

I had already served as the student-body president in both middle and high school, so I thought how crazy it would be if I were elected president of my college. I didn't tell many people about my dream, because I was afraid of what people might think. Fortunately, I didn't allow fear to deter me from going after my dream. Becoming president meant more to me than just a title; it would allow me the opportunity to give back to the college that I loved and make a difference for future students.

As the deadline approached for me to announce my candidacy, I was extremely nervous. Would people actually vote for me? As I began to tell people my plans, I gained a lot of support. I was already a personable and outgoing guy, so speaking to people was right up my alley. I ran for student-body president after I came back from studying abroad in South Africa. My campaign slogan was "United We Stand." I enjoy interacting with different groups, so I thought a slogan that reflected my stance on inclusiveness was most fitting.

Faced with the challenge of not knowing any of the new freshmen, I was already behind my opponents. I ran against three other guys: Gaston Albergotti, Jacob Godwin, and Tyrell Jemison. Gaston and Jacob were both involved in large fraternities on campus, and Tyrell knew just as many people as I did, so I knew it would be a tight race. I began campaigning a month before the election. I didn't want anything more than I wanted to be president. I spoke to people, met with groups, and got feedback from faculty and students alike. During that time, my schoolwork unfortunately took a backseat because I had an election to win.

The day of the election, I released the outcome into God's hands. Of course I was thinking I could have done more, but at that point there was nothing more I could do. The results came back, and there had to be a runoff between Gaston and me. The winner had to have over 51 percent of the votes. Gaston was a very tough competitor. He was an all-around good guy, and both of his older sisters had served as student-body presidents while they were Wofford students. We were given more time to campaign for the runoff election, but I still felt it was out of my hands at that point.

When the current president, Josh Turner, called and asked to meet with us to reveal the results before they were announced to the entire student body, I was extremely nervous. I was having dinner with two of my friends at the time. They knew how hard I had worked during my entire campaign, and knew how badly I wanted to be president. They were concerned about how I would react if I lost the election, so they tried to console me before the news even broke. Still, I had a good feeling! Josh asked Gaston and me to meet him outside the campus restaurant where I was eating with my friends. When I walked out of the restaurant, I immediately noticed Gaston walking up with three of his fraternity brothers. It looked like a gang was rolling up, but it wasn't anything like that. They were there for support. I hadn't asked my friends to join me because I wanted to break the news to them myself. When Josh told me I'd won, I could not believe it. I was elated! I walked back into the restaurant and let everyone know that I was the next student-body president. The room went crazy! People came up to me and congratulated me, and I was pulled in every direction.

I just wanted to call my mom. I ran outside, where it was quiet enough to call my momma. As excited as I was, I changed my tone to give her the impression I hadn't won. She answered, and I said, "Mom, guess what? I won the election." She repeatedly said, "No, you didn't." She quickly realized that I wasn't lying, and she couldn't have been any happier for me. It was one of the best moments of my life!

Your Dreams Are Worth the Fight

The dreams you have are given to you by God. The Bible says to "take delight in the Lord, and He will give you the desires of your heart," but you must first "commit your way to the Lord" (Ps. 37:4–5 NIV). I'm talking about the dreams that keep you up at night. The dreams that you believe in so deeply that no one can keep you from achieving them. If you are truly passionate about your dream, your dream is worth the fight.

What is meant for you will come to fruition. Do not be dismayed when it seems people around you are getting their big breaks when they haven't worked as hard as you have, or sacrificed as much. Wait on the Lord, because no sustainable success happens overnight. It takes dedication and hard work. In the thirty-seventh psalm, David writes, "Be still before the Lord, and wait patiently for Him; do not fret when people succeed in their ways when they carry out their wicked schemes" (Ps. 37:7 NIV). God didn't fight your battles to then leave you alone. The reason you are still here today is because God sees potential in you.

Pray this simple prayer to ask God for His guidance:

Lord, I pray for your guidance as I strive for my dream.
Lord, I ask that your will be done, and not my own.
If my dream doesn't align with your purpose for my
    life, I pray that you reveal to me your purpose so
    I can best be used by you.
In Jesus's name, I pray. Amen.

To fully live out your purpose, you have to have confidence in your own abilities. If you have drive, determination, innate ability, and Christ on your side, you can accomplish anything. If you don't believe you can do it, who will? It is disheartening to see people with so much potential squander their opportunities away. Maybe you've been caught in the quagmire of life. You know you're capable of doing more, but you don't have the confidence to follow through. I think the world is longing for your contribution. I cannot give you confidence—that comes from within—but I will say that life happens in a fleeting moment, and you deserve to live. God created you to live an abundant life, and this comes through following your dreams.

Life can really get the best of us sometimes. We wonder about the purpose of dreaming when we cannot escape our reality. Don't allow temporary distractions to keep you from your purpose. Visualize what you want to do with this one life you've been given. Some people choose to create a vision board. It's imperative that you do whatever you need to do to focus on your vision.

Each day, you should strive to be, and do, better. A company is not reliant on its past successes; the employees and employers challenge themselves to grow the brand. You have the opportunity each day to invest in yourself. Whether it's by laughing more, getting rid of negative people, or perfecting your craft, small steps like these will make a world of difference in your life.

Your youth is the best time to start. People are less likely to kill your dreams at an early age, but I'm not saying that it doesn't happen. When I was younger, I wanted to be an entrepreneur. I sold beaded key chains at one point, and gel candles at another. I believe people were more supportive of me because I was a kid. I would go from door to door in my neighborhood selling my products, and I would even send some to my mom's job for her to sell.

One particular customer at my mom's job bought one of the beaded fish key chains I had made. The customer liked the fish so much that she asked for another one just like it. That was great news until I realized I didn't have the same beads I'd used to make the first one, and I didn't remember the design of that first fish. I found a similar pattern and used the beads I already had. I sent the new fish to her, and she sent it back because it didn't look the way she wanted it to look. She wanted a replica of the one she had bought before. I gave her money back, and I apologized for not being able to fulfill her order, and that was it. My days as an entrepreneur were over.

This reminds me of how afraid I was to fail. Learn from my mistake, and trust yourself to handle failure. Failure will happen in business and in life, but we have to rebound from it. Each failure is a reminder of what we should do differently or change the next time around. You can handle failure and live through it. More often than not, the people whom we deem successful have failed at something. We don't often get to see the failures people have on their way to success.

For example, Tyler Perry, renowned playwright, director, and producer, posted a video called "How to be Successful" in which he talks about how he put on the same play every year for seven years before he was ever noticed. For the first six years, less than sixty people attended his shows, and they were usually family members and friends. He lost money on each show, but he didn't give up, and he is now living proof that you can excel beyond failure[1].

---

1 Tyler Perry, "How to Be Successful," YouTube, January 23, 2012, https://www.youtube.com/watch?v=QH0UoswCZ6w.

CHAPTER 5

ACTIVATE
YOUR FAITH

I tell you the truth, if you have faith as small as a mustard seed, you can say to this mountain, "Move from here to there," and it will move. Nothing will be impossible for you.
—Matt. 17:20 (MSG)

Any product produced by God is dependent upon God. God will not let any of His products lack the necessities they need to survive. Life is a process, and during each test or trial it becomes more and more evident which power source you're connected to. Oftentimes we may find ourselves synched to the wrong power source—sources that can only bring temporary satisfaction. The love of money, fame, and titles are examples of power sources that cannot be sustained. If you lose these things and you don't know who you are, then that's a problem.

All of the stuff you've accumulated is just that—stuff. What makes you really successful is doing what God has called you to do.

Don't Limit God's Power

The way God intends to bless you "no eye has seen—[and] no ear has heard" (1 Cor. 2:9 NIV). If you take a moment to think back over your life, you will see how God has brought you out of situations that seemed never-ending. God has infinite power, and He's not bound by previous blessings; how he blessed you before is no indication of how he plans to bless you in the future. Just have faith, and know that everything will work out for your good.

Activating your faith takes work. God's will sets the standard for how we should live our lives, but it requires work on our part. Nothing worth having in life comes easily. Yes, things would be easier if we could just snap our fingers, spin around three times, and request a blessing, but that's not possible. Even if it were possible, we wouldn't know how to manage all the stuff we've been given. God takes us through stages during which we learn and grow in preparation for the next level. Life is a never-ending stairwell that doesn't stop on the rooftop of perfection. Each staircase is a new stage of elevation in our efforts to be more like Christ. Although we can never be exactly like Christ, it's our constant striving and persistence that pleases God. No matter how high up on the stairwell we are during this Christian journey—or if we're still in the lobby—we are all works in progress. God's grace and mercy is sufficient to cover all of our shortcomings. Love, compassion, and respect are what we need to aid in one another's spiritual growth.

Whatever you envision for your future, you have to be reliant upon your faith in God to get you from one position to the next. God only wants the best for you, and you must trust Him through the process. Your faith is the key that unlocks all the blessings He has for you. You don't have to compromise your faith to excel in this world. If you had to cheat your way to the top, then it'll eventually catch up with you. Be patient with the process because elevation happens in stages, and some stages are lengthier than others.

Maximize Your Thinking

If you have a dream you think you can achieve by your own efforts, it's not a true dream. It is a task. A dream should frighten you, because you can't achieve it on your own. You need God's help. There is nothing more rewarding than accomplishing something that you worked hard for and strived to achieve.

What are you waiting for? You can't get to where you want to go if you haven't begun to try. Whatever is stopping you or causing you to think that you don't deserve a better life is a lie. God wants you to have an abundant life. While you're waiting on God to fulfill your dreams, God is waiting on you. When you put the work in and prove your dedication to your dream, then God will do the rest. No matter the profession, if someone doesn't put in the work to get a position, how can their work ethic be trusted in that role? Work toward your dreams as if your life depends on it!

Always make God a priority. When you are in a relationship with Christ, your journey becomes a little straighter, but you should nevertheless brace yourself for a bumpy ride. Life will never be completely smooth sailing, but with God as your captain, you can weather any storm. You can connect with God through prayer and through involvement in a ministry or a charitable organization that feeds your spirit. The work you do to help someone else will help you keep things in perspective.

After making time for God, then focus on your family. The reason so many marriages fail is because this area is often neglected. Fathers miss out on relationships with their sons, and mothers lose their connections with their daughters because they don't make time for them. The family is the physical manifestations of God's word on earth. Parents, you have the responsibility of shaping your children's lives. Empowerment begins in the home. Maybe your parents weren't the best role models, so you're not sure how to raise your own kids; trust God to show you the way. Your child shouldn't have to suffer because you suffered. Young people, God said in His word to honor your father and mother. Don't get mad at me for this, but when your parents discipline you, it's only because they want to see you go in the right direction. Any good parent wants the best for his or her children. Just as Christ corrects us when we sin, our parents want us to make better decisions because they see potential in us.

Finally, after you have attended to these areas, you can focus on your dreams and aspirations. Small steps toward your goals are more meaningful than doing nothing. If you value your dreams, you will make time for them. Whatever position you are in, never be satisfied. Aim for higher, and expand your dreams. Your job may only sustain you financially as you go after your dreams, but don't allow the stresses of work or school to discourage you. God says when you "have been faithful with a few things; I will put you in charge of many things" (Matt. 25:23 NIV).

Invest in Yourself

If you're activating your faith and you know the dreams you have in mind for yourself, find an internship or shadow someone in your chosen potential industry. Learn all you can about that particular industry before you pursue a job you may end up not liking. Job opportunities may even come out of your internship, so don't be afraid to invest in yourself. Although being an intern isn't the most glamorous role, and the compensation may only be invaluable experience, there's no better way to learn if you're actually interested in something.

When I was a senior in college, I wanted to set up an internship with Craig Melvin at MSNBC. Craig and I had only met once before then, but we shared several connections. His brother Rev. Lawrence Meadows is my pastor, and we were both graduates of Wofford College. Applying for an internship with MSNBC was an act of faith, but I knew the worst he could say was no. Craig agreed to allow me to intern with him for a month at his New York office.

MSNBC was the best internship I could have ever asked for. It was crazy to be surrounded by such accomplished individuals, from the producers to the camera people to the on-air personalities. I was able to interact with several NBC correspondents such as Joy Reid, Melissa Harris-Perry, Alex Witt, Ron Allen, T. J. Holmes, and of course, Craig Melvin. This experience only inspired me to work harder to someday have a broadcasting career.

Allow your faith to propel you to reach your dreams. What's important to you may not be important to everyone else, so you have to encourage yourself to continue. God wants to use your story to inspire others to have faith and trust His word. You will accomplish your dreams, but first you have to believe.

CHAPTER 6

MARKETING YOUR BRAND

Let your light so shine before men, that they may see your good works, and glorify your Father which is in heaven.
—Matt. 5:16 (KJV)

The best way to market your brand as a Christian is to love. God sent us into the world to be reflections of His love and to love others as we would ourselves. Yes, your individuality, personality, and appearance may suggest who you are, but your compassion toward others speaks volumes of who you represent. To love like Christ is to love without boundaries.

We live in an interconnected world, and it often seems that we've lost our moral fiber. It hasn't been lost, just covered with fear. We avoid having tough conversations by putting up walls of prejudgment or clinging to stereotypes. We don't want to seem accepting of someone's lifestyle if it's different from our own. There is no reason why we can't be participants in life and engage in conversations with people who aren't necessarily like us. This is how we adapt and grow as people. Mentally segregating people is not only unproductive, it's wrong. Your strong convictions may challenge or even inspire someone who has never thought of life the way you do, and vice versa. But you have to come from a place of love, and be willing to listen. The world is much larger and includes far more human beings than just those on your block or in your town. Your life is much richer when you have people in it who think or experience life differently than you. Embrace new people and grow as a person.

Display Your True Self

You are the perfect design of who God intended you to be. If you cannot love yourself first, there is nothing out there that will complete you or validate you. Drugs, alcohol, or promiscuity can bring you satisfaction for a moment, but as the high wears off, you'll be left with the same feelings you had before. That is definitely no way to live.

We have to respect ourselves enough to put our best foot forward; our bodies are our temples. The foods we enjoy, the clothes we wear, and the people we date are reflections of how we view ourselves. For instance, how you dress or look is often a way for people to immediately judge you. Unfortunately, not everyone will take the time to get to know you. You have to dress the way you want to be perceived. God knows your heart and is not impressed by how you look.

As Christians, we are not perfect, nor should we pretend to be. We are saved by grace. God plans to market and broadcast you to show others His saving grace and power. Your brand as a Child of God isn't necessarily written on your forehead for others to see, but it is displayed in the way you live your life. When positioning yourself as a Child of God, you are also presenting yourself as a product of grace. You are subject to the will of the Creator. However God intends to use you, you have to offer yourself as a vessel to be used for His glory.

The misconception we keep telling ourselves is that we have to fit within the confines of what someone else deems acceptable. It takes courage to be yourself, to go against the grain, and to seek a better life for yourself when others around you try to tear you down. To stand in your truth is a testament of your character. If you accept Jesus as your savior, you are a Child of God. This title carries a lot of weight because you're not your own; you live for the Lord. No, the path will not be easy, but—trust me—you'll win. Through every challenge, you will be victorious! Christianity doesn't stifle who you are as a person; it enhances it. What makes you valuable is your connection to Christ. God wants us to strive to be better each day.

God is calling a generation of people who are willing to live for Him. A generation that doesn't accept mediocrity. You are God's hope. The reason there is still hope in this world is because you exist. You may not see the end of the road now, but I promise if you surrender to God's will and let Him have His way, you'll be a lot better off. Don't fight it! I fought it for the longest time. You have the potential to be great. God doesn't use you for some self-servicing purpose. Your success is His success. He wants to see you live your best life. When you diligently seek Christ, he will bless you far more than you could have imagined.

The time for action is now! How unfortunate would it be for you to spend your entire life longing to achieve something, but never quite making it because you got in your own way. You don't have to figure it out on your own; opportunities start with a *yes*—*yes*, Lord, to your will, and *yes* to your way. Show the world what you're made of! Your identity can't stay within the confines of your mind. Allow God to use you in a miraculous way so others might see the goodness of our Lord. A life guided by God will end well. Better days are before you.

God says in Matthew 10:33 (NIV), "Whoever disowns me before others, I will disown before my Father in heaven." We have to be careful whom we let influence us. It's normal to want to fit in and to be liked by your peers, but at what cost? If your friends don't have a relationship with Christ, what does that say about you? It is imperative we acknowledge God and thank Him for His blessings. You may be quiet about your relationship with Christ around your friends, but there may come a time when you are tested and will find out which side you represent. To me, it's a no-brainer: I would rather live for Christ. You have a choice, and people are watching. If you begin to think for yourself and strive to live your best life, people may try to find ways to call you a hypocrite. They would rather see you act just like them. As I mentioned before, we aren't perfect, nor should we claim to be. We will probably make more mistakes than we can count, but we can get up every time. We are Children of God, and we are called for a higher purpose.

CHAPTER 7

BOUGHT AT
A PRICE

You are not your own; you were bought at a price.
—1 Cor. 6:19 (NIV)

Jesus made the ultimate sacrifice on Calvary for our sins. He gave His life so that we can have life in abundance. An abundant life can't be achieved on our own merits, but only by God's favor. God wants us to be blessed in all areas of our lives. Jesus assures us that our needs will be met because we were bought at the price of Calvary (Cor. 6:19 NIV). This analogy helps us understand that we belong to someone greater than ourselves, who has our best interests in mind.

In the Bible, Jesus often uses business terms to make his point. In Mark 8:36 (KJV), Jesus asks his disciples, "For what shall it *profit* a man, if he shall gain the whole world, and lose his own soul?" A profit is what is left over after debts have been subtracted from assets. In this analogy, Jesus emphasizes the point that it does not serve you any good to become successful and lose your integrity. You are spiritually unprofitable if you compromise your principles to gain something not ordained by God. You can scheme your way to success, but just as quickly as you achieved that small success, you will lose it.

When Jesus teaches us to pray in Matthew 6:12 (NIV), he says, "Forgive us our *debts*, as we forgive our debtors." Jesus teaches us to not be bound by apologies that we think we are owed. Someone may have robbed you of your joy, and the slightest thought of them is a constant reminder of that pain. Forgive them! If we are honest with ourselves, we all fall short when it comes to the Father, and we need Him to forgive us constantly. I would rather align myself with God than carry a grudge that just weighs me down. The perpetrator has likely gone on with their life. It's time for you to do the same.

Know Your Worth

You are so valuable that God does not give you what you deserve due to your sins, or burden you with more than you can handle. He will not leave you stranded to face the enemy on your own. How you view your situations should be the opposite of how you view your God.

Do you face big problems with a little god, or serve a big God who can easily handle your small problems?

What you are going through is not uncommon among others. We think our struggles are our own, and that no one could possibly understand. Often we give our life to our situations. We stress over these situations and cry over them, but those emotions soon consume us. We serve a God that is greater than any situation. What happens too often is that we perpetuate our situations out of fear. We stay in situations that break us down and damage our brand.

You may be in an abusive relationship, but you stay in that relationship because you don't feel you are worthy of being loved any other way. You feel like damaged goods. Do not devalue yourself prior to purchase. Jesus has already paid it all, and you are so precious to Him. If you are addicted to alcohol and/or drugs, you are also perpetuating the fear of not knowing how to let go of the disease. To completely remove yourself from addiction is scary because it has become a part of you. Do not be defined by the disease. Allow someone to help you overcome it.

God has loaned us these bodies, and His temple is inside of us. When we do harm to our bodies, we do harm to Him. Do not jeopardize your relationship with Christ just to get a quick fix. God does not deserve it, and you are worth more than that.

When I first gave my life to Christ, I was a bit naive. Honestly, I did it because I felt it was a prerequisite to becoming a gospel singer. As I grew older, life began to take a toll on me. I knew that I needed God more than ever. After being told so many times who I wasn't, I needed God to tell me who I was. My teenage years were a time of exploration. I started drinking alcohol, and I even tried smoking cigarettes and marijuana. I didn't do all this for me, but because of someone else. I don't want to deflect any responsibility, because I made the ultimate decision, but I know I did these things to fit in with my friends.

I often tried to live other people's truths. I remember playing on the basketball team in middle school and over-hearing my teammates talk about their "sex-capades." I felt I was behind, so I often lied about having sex. For all I knew, they were probably lying, too.

When you're ready, you will know. It's best to share that experience with your husband or your wife. You'll be pressured to do things that your peers are doing, but fight against the need to impress others. The most at-tractive and bold thing anyone can do is stand up for what they believe in and make their own decisions. No one can value you the way you can value yourself. When you know that you matter and should be respected, the world has no choice but to honor that.

Our reality—mine included—is such that we spend too much time concerned with other people's opinions. We look to find validation from people who don't see value in us unless we're giving them something. Have respect for yourself, and trust yourself. Maybe that group of friends you're hanging out with doesn't have anything nice to say, and they aren't the right friends for you. You shouldn't feel like you have to be in a certain position just because it's convenient. It would be unfortunate to be caught up in a situation that wastes your time and doesn't make you better as a person.

Relationships are designed for you to grow. When you're in a relationship that you know is right for you, you are challenged and inspired to work harder to ensure that the relationship thrives. This is not limited to romantic relationships; it pertains to friendships as well. The group of people you hang out with is a reflection of who you are. They will either make you better, or they will make you worse.

Selling Yourself Short

Never sell yourself short. When you give in to sin, you are selling yourself short. We will be impacted by sin as long as we are on this earth. We all fall short of the glory of God, but having the strength to get back up again indicates how much we value ourselves. Don't allow the environment you grew up in, or the trials life has dealt you, to limit you from achieving greatness. You are worth a great life, and it is up to you to decide how to use it. If you allow petty things to steal your joy, then you are living with a limited mindset. You can't be so complacent and simpleminded that you prevent yourself from experiencing all the wonders life has to offer. Dream big! If you have a dream, work as hard as you can to achieve that goal. You have the drive and the talent inside of you. Be invested in that dream so no hater, no test score, no financial issue, and no friend can deter you from achieving that goal. I know you can make it. God has already promised you victory, and if you trust Him, your next days will be your best days.

God has placed dreams inside of you so you can bring them to fruition. Don't allow something God has given you to take a backseat to your current situation. When God gives us an assignment, He forms a partnership with us. His part is already done, and He is just waiting on us to do ours. How important are your dreams? How important is it for you to do God's will? If you allow life's distractions to rob you of what God has already ordained for you, then you will not be successful.

Know who you are. You can't find real success if you do not have a sense of your identity. What makes you unique will be that thing that gets you the next job or your next relationship. Do all you can do to better yourself. If that means going back to school, starting your own business, or getting into shape—do it for yourself. You have all it takes to be successful inside of you. It's up to you to decide how badly you want it. You will win!

CHAPTER 8

SENT BACK TO THE MANUFACTURER

And the God of all grace, who called you to His eternal glory in Christ, after you have suffered a little while, will himself restore you and make you strong.

—1 Pet. 5:10 (NIV)

Jesus will always be there for you, even when you lose your way. I lost my way, and no matter how damaged of a product I became, I was always able to go back to the Manufacturer. We have a lifetime warranty with the Manufacturer because His grace is sufficient to cover any of our shortcomings. All of our past mistakes are history when we turn our lives over to Christ. We were created to be dependent upon him, because he knows us better than we know ourselves. If anything is broken, he knows exactly where to start the repairs. You can't make it alone in this world. You need something greater than yourself to guide you through the hard times, setbacks, and obstacles.

Making it in this world is tough. Greatness is achieved by those who are willing to work hard and take risks for what they love. If you falter or come short of your goals, find comfort in knowing that the Manufacturer will cover the rest.

Don't Feel Limited by Past Mistakes

Mistakes have a way of revisiting us in our weakest moments. Their return is a psychological ploy designed to destroy our faith when we're most vulnerable. How can we possibly move forward in life when a mistake we've made is our Achilles's heel? You must first address that issue. You cannot fix anything that you aren't willing to acknowledge. If you are afraid of what this mistake may say about you, you will lose your mind trying to suppress it. Release whatever is holding you back from fulfilling your destiny. You can share your story with a family member, pray, or write it down to get it out of your system. You are perfect the way God made you, and He allowed for that mistake to happen. He wants to use this experience as a teachable moment to assure you that He will always be there for you. All you need to do is call on Him when you need Him. Your purpose doesn't end with the mistakes you've made. It begins when you allow God to direct your path.

Being sent back to the Manufacturer should not be seen as punishment, but as a time for you to be pulled aside and advised by the CEO. It's comforting to know that God cares enough for you that He is willing to correct you and steer you in the right direction. No, being corrected isn't fun, but it's necessary. If we were allowed to do whatever we wanted, there wouldn't be a place for God. Allow God to teach you and be your guide.

No matter how far off course you've gotten, you can still be sent back to the Manufacturer. God's return policy is a 100-percent-forgiven guarantee. You have to take control of your life and the choices you make in order to be elevated to new levels. You must alter your thinking. God is not surprised by anything you've done in your life. He's more concerned about whether you're willing to learn from your mistakes. If you're constantly doubting yourself, hanging out with the wrong crowd, and doing the same things you've been doing, then you won't grow and become the person God intended for you to be. You can't continue to do the same things and expect a different result. We all make mistakes, but no mistake should hold us back from our destiny.

I'm humbled when I'm sent back to the Manufacturer. During this time, it helps me realize that God is the only help I need. God allowed what we are going through to happen. It's not that He likes to see us suffer; instead, He loves us so much that he knows how to grab our attention. He wants to reconnect with you and build on your relationship. When you are in constant communication with the Father, you are surrendering to the will of God. You can't go wrong!

It's Your Time

There's nothing more liberating than being you. You cannot force it because the resulting happiness can only flow from within. Take the journey of self-discovery and fall in love with you. If you don't first love yourself, you won't have a reference point for how others should love you. Home in on those talents that make you unique. When you allow other people's opinions to deter you from your dreams, you are giving them control of your future. Go after your dreams, and you will be successful.

The hand of God is guiding your product through the assembly line of life. All of the hurt, trials, and tests prepare you for what God has in store for you. Without the proper testing, you would crash under pressure. The Manufacturer designed you to be strong and to withstand the tough times. Don't lose faith! God will always be there for you!

This life is short, and the time for action is now. Don't allow someone to persuade you to think that you're a failure, not good enough, or will never amount to anything. Yes, I heard these comments, and I allowed them to get me down, but despite it all, God continues to guide me to become the man He would have me be. Release the reins of guilt, shame, defeat, and your past mistakes to God, and allow Him to direct your path. Go out and show the world the best you that you can be.

No matter how you began in this life, there is success waiting for you. If you didn't have a purpose, you would never have been created. I'm excited for your future. Go get what God has promised you!

ABOUT THE AUTHOR

Ron Norman was born and raised in Woodruff, South Carolina. He is a graduate of Wofford College, where he served as student-body president and a Bonner Scholar. He is also a member of Phi Beta Sigma Fraternity, Inc. He is currently employed as a web content coordinator for CBS affiliate WSPA, where he started his own segment called "Taking It to the Street."

Norman is a member of New Bethel Baptist Church in Woodruff; while living and working in Atlanta, Georgia, he moved his membership by letter to House of Hope Atlanta, where he served on the media ministry. He has spent years motivating and inspiring young people to step into their destinies to fulfill their purposes in life. When asked to speak at different programs, his message is always simple: Never give up!

www.iambrandu.com
Twitter: @Ron_Norman2
Instagram: @iamronnorman

www.ingramcontent.com/pod-product-compliance
Lightning Source LLC
LaVergne TN
LVHW021409080426
835508LV00020B/2523